Northern Lights

Harry Gallagher

Stairwell Books

Published by Stairwell Books

161 Lowther Street
York, YO31 7LZ

ISBN: 978-1-939269-61-4

Second printing

Printed and bound in the UK by Imprint Digital
Layout design: Alan Gillott
Cover Photograph: *Blast Furnace at Redcar* courtesy Paul Kitchener

This book is dedicated to the memory
of Harry & Margaret Gallagher

Acknowledgements

Some of these poems were first published by Black Light
Engine Room, Lucifer Press, The Fat Damsel, Mary Evans
Collection, The Font, Northern Correspondent, Three
Drops from the Cauldron, Stare's Nest, Clear Poetry, Rebel
Poetry and Northern Writes.

Introduction

Teesside. Birthplace of intrepid explorer Captain James Cook; home to Gertrude Bell, a remarkable and pioneering woman who helped map the middle east as we now know it: footballing giants and arch rivals Don Revie and Brian Clough were born streets apart in its smoky centre; and we'll skip over the mighty parmo, The World's Least Healthy Dish.

It's said that in the mid-1800s, Middlesbrough resembled a smoke blackened Wild West. There were bars on literally every corner and lawlessness was rife. The work – iron foundries, shipbuilding, docks, chemical works – was dangerous and hard. People lived, understandably, in fear of the workhouse, a corrupt and death ridden hellhole for its unfortunate inhabitants.

Yet from all of this a culture was born. Now, mention the words 'Middlesbrough' and 'culture' together and you may receive snorts of derision (the loudest being from Boro people themselves), but Middlesbrough does have its own unique culture. In many ways, it's typified by the aforementioned Clough. We are chippy non conformists. Each funny remark disguises a hand grenade. A friendly wave, as often as not, has two fingers to the forefront. From generation to generation, red and white clad fathers pass on their pearls of wisdom: "The Boro'll always let you down, son."

But beneath all these forbidding appearances you will find the most solid, loyal, proud and hard-working folk you're ever likely to meet.

So all those people, all that work ethic... what happens to it when there is no work? We're all familiar with the changes wrought by our current postindustrial landscape, but in case you're under 40 here's a wee stat to give you a rough guide. When this poet left school in 1979 there were, from memory, some 45,000 people directly employed by British Steel on Teesside.

We now no longer make steel, the blast furnace having been sacrificed in return for Chinese help building a nuclear power plant elsewhere. And all under the baleful gaze of the minister for the laughable Northern Poorhouse project, unbelievably a local MP. This 45,000 loss is on top of the perished shipyards and downsized chemical industries.

So where did they all go, all those people who built bridges and ships the world over? They followed the example of their forefathers and became migrants themselves. I challenge you to step onto an oil or gas platform anywhere in the North Sea or Middle East and just listen. Within minutes your ears will be assaulted by that gruff twang – a "Now then chor!" or perhaps "Yer jokin' arn yer!" It's how we roll – all around the globe. I have encountered my townsfolk in most countries in Europe, in Kazakhstan, in Qatar, in fact everywhere I have worked. We are a mongrel town and it suits us well.

For those of us lucky enough to have roots, our hometowns are often what make us. Teesside runs through this book like the mighty Tees thunders down the face of High Force. Did I mention by the way, how stunningly beautiful our area is? Best not, we don't want to be overrun by southerners! See what I mean about our loveable, passive aggressive ways?

Harry Gallagher

Come with me, see the Northern lights;
feel a ragged wind blow
as we waltz between snow heavy clouds,
tracing treetops as we go.

Come with me where sky meets sea
and the world goes on forever,
stretching out her barley skin;
shelter for we driftwood to abide in.

So hold on fast and brave the brace
of a million crashing, cleansing waves
then dry your body in the warming rays
of the kinder Northern lights. //

Table of Contents

Chapter 1 – Father Time

Ghost River

Cobbling over Hadrian's trod,
going back, back, back
to river's edge. Gulls idly
chatter with herons on bones
of conveyors, cranes, staithes
lodged in silt, water topped up
with ancient stevedore blood.

Ships playing pretend
that the old girl
is still thriving. Alive
with cries and roaring chains,
as virgin hulks slipaway
to Valparaiso or Cairo.

Off to countries never seen
by alchemists who hammered
shape into giants. ⚒

St Mary of the Lighthouse

St Mary lives in a lighthouse,
where peels of paint
give up the ghosts
of faint fishing fleets.

She sings her laments to baby
seals, newly furred against
Baltic breeze; a twirling ballerina
in her lonely spyglass world.

A holy military lookout
for long forgotten sailors,
palming boats away from boulders
and calming pounding hearts.

She sleeps on seashell pillows,
starfishing atop the bedrock.
On awakening, the sand is rubbed
soft from her eyes.

And twice a day, when spies
are tidied from the island,
she waltzes lovely in the surf,
blowing kisses out to the horizon. ⁄⁄

Newport Staithes

The groaning of iron on your sides
and a river's filth in your mouth
has seared sludge into your grains.
The might of a world now gone;
licked black then belched back
by a careworn hag who'd had enough.

Poor waterless gypsy mares
staring ironic with pity
at the burnt bloody sailor
drank legless and lame;
clinging grimly to the bank,
bearing tales of wild old days.

So bolt down the bridge to ships,
whose spirit shapes will come no more.
Lift the very last plates from the press,
the time for lifting is gone. ⁂

The Zeppelin's Biggest Mistake

On 14th April 1915, a German Zeppelin ghosted in over Blyth in Northumberland and began dropping incendiaries over various locations, mostly landing in fields etc. It then made its way to Wallsend and dropped one on the house of a woman bathing her young daughter. Local defense volunteers opened fire on it with rifles, whereupon it retreated back out to sea.

Howay ower the Tyne
with your bombs bonny lad,
bring that fat old balloon overhead.
This is the town that Hadrian built;
we pulled down his wall,
we'll take you down an' all.

Only I wouldn't linger long if I were you,
because me and me mates
are primed with wor rifles.
See, you went too far last night
when you slipped your filthy bombs
on Mrs Robinson's house;
her little lassie in the bath,
oil bubbling through rafters.

The fire is out now,
you mightn't like to hear.
Bairns safely out on cobbles,
she strode back into flame
and flannelled away
the last traces of you.
See, this is what happens
when the devil hangs around
in cloud ower God's country.
Angels like her tell devils like me,
casting upwards to Heaven
with Hell in me fingers.

So don't stay away too long bonny lad,
steer that big black bumblebee
ower here where we can see it.
We are men who magic up ships,
our fists pull coal from the earth
and I've shit bigger than you.

I'm gannin' back to the missus
and bairns now son,
and ye gan back to yours.
But don't stay away
and don't be a stranger;
we'll keep the home fires burning
and I've got one here for you! ⁄⁄

Big Geordie

Pitprop legged,
he strides the tides
of a brimming river.

Slackblack skinned,
he slyly winks
and claims both sides.

Bulkheaded, mighty,
fights passing chancers.
Gives praise weekly
at St James' temple.

Misty lidded at
the mention of
his lost love Mauritania;

she was built by the book,
an ogress whose bed
was sliced through The Wall.

His fists grip the bridges
like bracers to his pants,
sees skeletons of cranes
kidding on they're alive.

And on sunny days,
he can see the seaside,
but he is a city boy,
where his jackhammer heart
pummels his veins.

Each beat an ocean,
shovelled up in his hands
to make rain for the parched,

who cower 'neath the arches
of the railway King,
one time pretender
to the throne.

He speaks the Queen's English,
loves his old mam
and sings in tones
that only the noble can hear. ⁄⁄

Mr Panico

In wartime Middlesbrough, as soon as Italy declared war on Britain, the previously loved ice-cream family, the Panicos, began having their windows put in.

Today's ice-cream may contain
hundreds and thousands,
somewhat sharp on the tongue.
A shard 99 special.

As old Mr Panico combed
the remains of his windows
out of his scalp, the cares
of the world came to rest

on the shoulders of a sudden
accidental outsider, as a town
full of mongrels turned
on the little man who had made
their own children's lives
that wee bit sweeter. ⁄⁄

Evacuee

Stand there! they said;
lined up for inspection.
Unfresh from the carriage
into a twilight schoolhall,
lined up for inspection.

And the last child standing
was branded for life
by the horrorstruck
looks from the farmer
and his berry faced wife.

So the shortstraw urchin,
head hanging, trailed forward,
matchstick legged,
fingernails packed tight
with all the tar
the ironmasters could muster.

It was all enough to set
his face against want
and accidents of birth
roadmapping lives.

The reason fading films
show him sandcastling on beaches,
suited, tied up by the looks
from the kindest strangers
who took in a lost boy
and sent home a man. //

Autumn Sunday

The ambering of leaves,
sucked anaemic by season;
the ghost of Derwentcote
haunts a field gone doleful.

The forest's path, still hiding
a railway's lost foundations;
slippery fingers to trip ponies
heaving up the iron.

Sidings surrendered to brambles,
the year's final pickings
lightfingered like sweeties
from slumbering children.

And onwards to Earsdon's
village of the dead,
a monument to obsolescence;
boys of ten laid beside old men.

New Hartley, Backworth,
Blue Bell, dear old Maude
knew what we have forgotten:
time reclaims all her precious jewels. ⁄⁄

The Ghosts of Hester

There are voices around the capped off shaft,
ghosts of gatherers weighing in the coal.
The tallylad, the stopper – a blackfaced bairn
drowned in his dad's coat, fists knuckling through sleeves.

All waiting for the menfolk to fashion a ladder
from brittle ferrous flakes embedded in the walls
and climb out into the Heaven of a January morning,
crisp as starched sheets on a dead man's bed.

But everybody knows about the fathers who held sons,
suffocating them with love to save the gas a job.
Where little boys were found in the snuggled underground,
grasping daddy's gasping chest, is plotted now on maps.

As deep as the waters drowning the main seam,
their shade is absorbed in the existence of a people
who just chose the wrong time and place to be born.

They now wander a garden they don't recognise,
filled up with words that cannot convey
the weight or the reach of a snapped beam's fist.

And so here they still dwell, moaning the names
of the spared twenty five. Faint as a boy's imprint
sitting against a coalface at a sleepy last supper,
praying for a miracle that never appeared. ⁄⁄

Sinking

Who remembers you now, Mary Isabella?
Darling George, whose fingers straightened
your Sunday bonnet straws, no longer
parts the ivy on top of your headstone.

Taken at forty by the Lord at Church Pit;
not your children either,
Cradled into the earth as babes,
Tuberculosis' little coughdrops.

All these sons and daughters
of Hartley Old Engine, West Farm,
being swallowed in death
by what took them in life.

Bones backfilling the hateful hollows
they themselves dug out, as the coaly
caverns take everything back beneath
a greening Northumberland churchyard. //

Chapter 2 – Walking Out

Spinning the plates

Echoes of teenage Sunday mornings
vacuum their way across time and space,
and the smell of a bubbling roast
headswims through the decades.

Potatoes peeled and pan bound,
the rumble of sofa being shifted
while acute adolescent boredom
melted bleary bodies onto beds.

Wife at church, you worshipped
in your own slice of heaven,
your only half day of rest spent
happily spinning the plates. ⁄⁄

Rosemary

Before we sprouted and grew,
there was Rosemary; a ghost
of a little girl, lost
in the concrete and bricks

of an orphanage meadow.
A little flower ever unpicked
among the remembrance
and forget-me-nots.

Unloved and untended,
save for a childless couple,
desperate to harvest
their lovely empty garden.

Whatever the reason,
the Sisters Of No Mercy
at Nazareth House
lived up to their name
and were stone steadfast:

You must break contact.
Too close to adopt.
Too loving.

By some miracle of nature, the loss
of Rosemary was our gain, as we
came along, perennial;
rooting in heartbreak soil.

So we grew with a missing sister;
as until the day she died,
a small corner of my mother's
flowerbed was forever Rosy. ⁄⁄

Our Nanna's House

Our nanna's house smells funny
an' grandad's only got one eye.
He needs a shave but his face shakes
an' I'm too shy to ask why.

An' nanna's laid up on the settee
dyin' for want o' some stout,
but our dad's just slipped her 50p
and now she can't wait to get us out.

An' she's on her feet, a whirlwind
not much bigger than me.
Back in the car, mam says
it's a miracle recovery.

* * * * *

Long before we're tucked in bed
nanna's on the bottles of black,
jigging away on the tables,
grandad quivering in the sack.

Dreaming of home over the Irish Sea,
fit as a goat, shovel in hand;
before he broke his body, laying
tarmacadam across the land.

Nanna's hiding inside the bottle
where the sisters cannot find her,
drowning in shame at the sound of her name,
the ghosts just a step behind her.

Our nanna's house smelled funny
and grandad had just the one eye,
an empire's poorest children
crushed beneath a soot filled sky. ⫽

Clackers Are Crackers!

A gentle man in gentle times; kindness
and standards and tales of old days.
Of tawses used to blister small hands,
those welts still real in your mind's eye.

Now standing on stage, assembling the lines;
jollying smiles playing on your face.
And today's theme is a cautionary tale
of what happens to children in the latest craze.

How shattered hardstone
would polish corneas
and broken bones leave
fingers hanging limp.

Clackers are crackers!
You beamed at your line
and Miss Cassidy chuckled
at the softest of heroes. ⫻

Two Boys Play in Evening Sea at Cullercoats Bay

No notion that they
are making memories
to last the rest
of their livelong days
(and why would they?)

No vision of the shadows
of lost waggonways,
nor the artists' colony
that once coloured Bank Top.

No idea the middle age spread
men with children
(that they will surely become)
will look back on these nights
with salting eyes,
wondering where the years went.

They see only the depths
of the harboured sea,
holding their forevers
around them. ⟋

What You Smelled Of

Stewed meat and pastry
and carrots and gravy
and potatoes and engines
and grease and oil
and sweat and toil
and a vest stuck to
a wheezy chest
and knees to sit on
and shoulders for small heads
and a voice that sang
The Skye Boat Song.
One line and I'm gone.
Speed Bonnie Boat... //

Square

Wide eyed, benign; body inclined
in a self conscious gesture
to somehow include
the outofsorts child
masquerading in the skin
of his bumbledown boy.

Arched over the bonnet
of the latest edition
of door to door runarounds
which keep his wife mobile,
all attempts to pique interest
join the oil on the floor.

Lumpen, the son sees shapes
form on the lips of his dad.
Hears a strange foreign tongue;
remains resolutely square
in a big round world, drowns
in the sounds playing in his head.

The chasm between them will
one day close. But for now,
over sympathy and swarfega,
he hears: *He'll have to find
non manual work. Perhaps
something in an office.* ⫽

Hell's Supernun

Too vindictive to be just any figure of fun;
a vision of fury was Hell's Supernun.

Beating ten year olds with shoes, lumps of wood;
she'd thrash the parents too if only she could.

Unholy churchbound Sundays, from yawning dawn til dark,
each missing child received a place in her tarred heart.

And when those names matched ones she already hated,
they'd be splayed and displayed and humiliated.

Each dreadful weekday they'd drag their poor skins in,
these *dirty creatures* born from original sin.

Mothers kept at bay by a jolly shamrock smile;
cheeks flowering roses, tongue made of bile.

Brain of burning coal, eyes throwing fire;
hands forged from iron, fingers twisted wire.

No parent would believe what all we children knew –
the colour of Catholicism was vivid black and blue. ⧸⧸

Terence

When I was at school, perfecting
the fine art of disappearing;
blending into blackboards, coat pegs,
white lined tarmac and the bonding
to be had in inventing nicknames,
there you were. Ill fitting the backdrop;
a boy's clothes not disguising
a voice and a manner which left you
no hiding place.

Sashaying in a hothouse
for the dragons it bred;
deliberately provoking
each beating you took.
Refusing to fit in with the rest,
who knew by instinct where
the invisible line was –
we picked it up and towed it.

Years later, long escaped,
I heard about you from my mum:
That Terence – he drowned in a canal, you know.
Well he was always a queer sort.

The Following Moon

As a boy, carbound and sped,
I was taken by the notion
that attached to our back bumper
was a moon magnet.

Whole forests would branch past,
the car gobbling up tarmac;
one rearwindow glance and...
...yep. Still there.

Stuck only on us,
it jetted through clouds,
playing mum's Morris 1100
at cat's eyes dominos.

And there it still is,
peek-a-booing in the nightsky;
dependably devoted, dragging
its tides behind it. ⁄⁄

Pocahontas

My father had a secret love
before mother came along;
he told us all about her,
with Mam shaking her head
under a killjoy standard lamp.

But before she could stop him
the truth was blurted out:
as a lad, our Dad had
shared a bed with Pocahontas!

The youngest daughter's doubts
were quickly drowned out
by the proof on his upper arm:
a smallpox needle's scar.

But not inoculation, it transpired.
No! The mark of an arrow fired
from the trusty bow of a dusky squaw
who played Cupid with our Dad!

But why did she leave?
the five year old girl asked.
Oh, I couldn't get to sleep –
her feathers tickled me nose.

The next day the tale
was tall all over school,
of how a Middlesbrough fitter
had tasted glamour and glitter
but left it all for the high life. //

Softlad

Softlad yearns to disappear –
to be devoured by corners,
swallowed whole by wallpaper.
For carpets to fly him away
through thick jet clouds,
filling out the flesh
hanging scruffy from bones,
mumbling at the day.

Softlad dreams in off white,
where time is galumphing
and language is garbled
by a tongue gone to treacle.
And sotto voce is reserved
for imagined lovers,
as the mirror glares back
the enemy of love.

One day postwar schoolrooms
will never find him again,
where spitfire teachers,
two pints worse at lunchtime,
unsteadily perch on desk edges;
unsure where the boy
who would get nowhere
has finally sloped off to. ⫽

Shirleen, Sixteen

Shirleen, sixteen;
fearsome Amazon,
pregnant for the third time.

Insecure bullyboy
preaching teacher,
searching for a scratching post
on which to mark his patch
and impress an elder
Statesman Of Sadistry.

His eyes light feverly
as they alight eagerly
on the big black girl
at the back of the class,
who is looking outside
at a future made from
cots, kids, blokes
who will come and go,
then mid 30s grannydom.

Shirleen Boyce!
The soundwave slaps her
back to the now
and the quivering thin man,
looming overhead,
stick aloft, shaking delighted.

Put out your hand, girl!
He is smacked in the ears by:
Fuck. Off.

Pride smithereened
and elder hovering
like a Summersick wasp,
the cane descends full force.

By lunchtime everyone knew the story,
growing exponentially,
of how Wanker Watson
had picked on The Wrong One.

How the girl/woman
had snatched the weapon
from his desperately sweaty grasp
and returned it full force.

And how with one mad act,
a baleful monster
had its bubble pricked
by Shirleen, sixteen. ⁄⁄

Independence Hill

The never get out of bed boy
got out of bed today
and an alarmed mum
tearfully reset her clock,
as the second hand snailed
slowly towards progress.

And as he fell into
the open embrace
of a forever grateful
never give up teacher,
he blew his absent father
the ghost of a Teesside kiss.

Striding manfully away
from Lost Boy Avenue,
his coat zipped up
against frozen wastes,
he commenced the long slow climb
towards Independence Hill. ⟍

Chapter 3 – Out in the Middle

Jack

The shipyards turned out Jack
and Jack turned out a family:
three boys and three girls
with a matriarch made of steel,
who taught him how to feel
like a motherless child.
So each night, a gallon of mild
sank its way through the skin
that he never learned to live in.

Between the clanging of rivets
and the haranguing of the wife,
the pickling process
eased an unbearable life;
where for a boy with
gossamer paper for skin,
a house doused in flame
held no corners to hide in.

So Drinking Jack
turned Shrinking Jack.

From the ship to the boozer
to the asylum of an armchair
in a dying living room,
he's brylcreemed to perfection
and he dresses to thrill.

Inside the mind of a man
who hides from the drill
of an overbearing woman
who goes in for the kill;
who needed a father
but married a boy,
so she throttled him dry
of every ounce of joy
until he drank and drank and drank. //

Café Moment

Man stood up while sitting down.
Madeoflove mother with daughter
coffeeing opposite, sunrays lightening
already barley hair. She catches the whiff
of alone. Glances. Knows what to do.

Her reachacross hand pats his sunken
sternum, with all the delicacy of nurture.
Eyes touch in line. Silentsoft kindsmile
passes on unspoken *It'll be ok, you'll see.*

A forever moment, before time
untangles itself. No sepia spoiling words.
A nod, a final touch and a lighter
walkaway than he dared dream. ⁄⁄

This is How I Fell

Buying shoes for the bairn –
this is how I fell.

Missing a gas instalment –
this is how I fell.

Having a cardiac arrest –
this is how I fell.

Being born in the wrong country –
this is how I fell.

Losing my lovely wife –
this is how I fell.

Redundant at 55 –
this is how I fell.

Getting kicked out for coming out –
this is how I fell.

Always needing one more drink –
this is how I fell.

And I fell and I fell;
and when I fell,
my safety net, being full of holes,
couldn't catch me.

So I fell onto the street,
with a bench for a bed
and a park for a house
and frostbite for comfort
and derision for food
and spit from a stranger for drink.

And a disappeared life. //

Song

The air is scimitared
by the cobalt and zest
of a kingfisher's crest;
but the only sound
worth hearing in town
is the dreamtime song
of the blackbird. ⁄⁄

Sunday Morning, Longsands

Though the mist crawls in
on an invisible tide
and the sun is a ghost;
undeterred and resolute,
children soldier on.

Boys chase each other
across sandy trenches,
trusty swords in hands,
while little girls signal
in a series of screams.

Each squeal a dash,
every shout a dot,
relayed to the pierhead,
which returns its low moan.

And life carries on,
each of us in our bubbles,
borne along atop surf
on a tiny blue dot. ⁄⁄

Heart of The City

Idling on the spikes
of global corporations,
sanctioned to standstill,
they swap stories, crutches
and heavensent substances,
dulling the winds
that whip off the canal.

Swaddled in the rags
of what once was a parka,
a hand me down girl,
landed down on the kerb,
fits in with the hoodies,
newfound bosom buddies
and the drugs do the rest.

Each doorway a sob
waiting for a sleeve;
suffer little children
with nothing to believe. ⁄⁄

The Oily Sea

Back and forth, back and forth;
on and off, on and off.

And the galvanized stairs
accept the footfall
of the family man
sucked in by the call
of the oily sea, the oily sea.

Back and forth, back and forth;
on and off, on and off.

And the carpeted stairs
and artexed ceiling
are ruled by the wife
he now sees as unfeeling,
who was suckered by dreams
now long drowned
in the oily sea, the oily sea.

Back and forth, back and forth;
on and off, on and off.

And time on the shore
is now spent drinking
and warring over
territories shrinking.

And the unspoken thoughts
she guiltily dreams
are of days before they came
apart at the seams;

before they knew nothing
ever comes for free,
when they sold their souls
to the oily sea. //

41

Autumn Sonnet

As nature sheds her coat of gold
and turns to brown beneath the feet,
the signs outside the church read *Sold*
and Autumn's mist reclaims the street.
A man of God widens his stride,
dog collar tightened, sweating brow'd;
his greatcoat flapping, ripped awide,
his throbbing heart booms faith aloud.
He counts each step, and each in time;
missing the cracks, catching his breath.
Clapping eight syllables per line,
playing it cool, catching his death.
The chaotic everyday, so repulsive
to God's unholy obsessive compulsive. ⁄⁄

Angel
For p.a.morbid

He tracks the trails of the river
and the trickling of time,
trawls by the terraces
of an unemployed working town
and finds magic in the cracks.

Sees Quaker bricks bearing
fingerprints of outsiders;
these bridge builders who played
jointhedots across a globe,
smaller now than it was.

Headstones are logged:
marble, stone, iron, still
spattered from the works.
Reads strange immigrant names,
forgers of a future now passed.

Allthewhile, blackwings feather
the frontage of borders
invisible to him. Each turn
of the light noted captive
in a pocketbook for nightfall. ⁂

Unlived

The riot of steel
and the debasing of men
who know better.
Outside, the shock absorber
doubling as a door
keeps time with the rate of cells
perishing in this withering frame.

Where hope and ambition
exist only outside gates
corroded by the rain
spearing down outside and in.

And time, that thieving charlatan,
will give nothing back for this;
where we all earn the pittance to pay
for dreams which will stay unlived. ⁄⁄

From a Window

Double decker faces,
pressed against glass;
pressed for time.
It's sundown in
the seaside town.

Sun slinking down
in the humdrum world
of the busy commuter;
each a story to live,
and miles and years to go. //

Zorro

In Newcastle this morning
a giant rainbow zedded itself
lazily across a brace of clouds.

God's been up all night,
playing at being Zorro again. ⁄⁄

Bongo

It's all in the offbeat.
Dancefloor quaking beneath the feet
of a Friday night.
Beats ringing from Kingston
and the feel of the Windrush
pushing you on to
Get up! Stand up!
Stand up for your rights!

And though Marley is righteous,
the fight just left you
and you're smiling instead.
Now Prince Buster's in your head
and Rico's in your shoes,
rocksteadying your legs,
man you just can't lose.

And the walls are sweating
out the regrets
of fifty years of drunken punters
who were shunted outside
to the freezing night air
of a steelheaded town.

No welcome there,
except the spirits of sailors
who landed up unlucky
and left behind their DNA
in the heartbeat of the shack
where the beats are black
and no quarter is given
in a joint that's riven

with streetgirls and lager louts
and cast offs and cast outs,
who went home on ships,

tales dripping from their lips
about the things they saw,
the memories they built,
the legends born
and the blood that was spilt
at Club Bongo International. ⁄⁄

How it is

Breathe in, breathe out, keep walking.

That's you and me in that picture,
framed in our annual *how it is* moment.
Catching each other up, while dodging
the glare of the works, pouting
at having to light up on Boxing Day.

Breathe in, breathe out, keep walking.

And our warm exhalations mix with
the calico clouds from South Gare,
bonding with the sky, as gulls fly by
crying at the spilling of secrets
and the dropping of bombshells on sand.

Breathe in, breathe out, keep walking.

And for an hour we flow wild like tide,
surfing the quarries and peaks of our lives.
one of us leaning, the other carrying;
and we never know which will be which
until the day arrives and we empty
our spoil to the sea. ⁄⁄

The Morning After

Fret frozen city Sunday,
shops shuttered to save
you from meeting your
own cruel reflection.
Head down as if a hundred
marshland miles to go.
Nothing looks the same
the morning after.

Last night's fruit,
suddenly turned from
forbidden juicy July
into bitter November raisins
strewn about the kerb,
side by side with wrappers
and half eaten meat,
waiting to be swept away
by sickly lime hi viz men.
No, nothing feels the same
the morning after.

The laughter forgotten, cast off
like the mask it always was.
Left behind, only the need,
the greed for flesh.
Oh to be wrapped up in the arms
of another hungry consumer,
another deluder to mirror
the hangover in waiting.
But nothing looks the same
the morning after.

And as the calendar turns
to Autumn's battleship grey
and sobriety, the reality
is of another hollow day.

Regretting the cheap lines
that the drink and you threw at her,
just to prove once again
that nothing looks the same
when you're trudging through
the morning after. ⁄⁄

Auntie Jean

Auntie Jean, archetypal warchild.
Came out fighting,
never really stopping;
bobbing and weaving,
never retreating
while the bombs were dropping.

Born under a swastika sky,
alive with fascistic fury;
clenched fists would never wander far
for the woman who spat fire at enemies within.

A nurse and a mother,
but all the time fighting,
igniting at the slightest hint.
The glint in her eye would light
and the pyrotechnical pilot
would be called to arms.

No battle too much
for the woman with the touch
of a flame thrower. ⁄⁄

TLF

All the joy of sunshine,
toasting green turf gold.
Tinkerbell's toes carrying
the dreams of thousands;

as on weekends for just
a twinkle of time,
grown men became boys,
grubby hands leafing comics.

And the blackeyed little town
suspended its heartbeat,
as the tiny magician
went native.

Men and women stared doe eyed,
if not at each other.
But no-one really minded,
united as they were

by this juggler of hopes,
this fairydust sprinkler,
as we all fell in love
together. ⁄⁄

Perfect Saturday

The spears of
a fret strewn Saturday
are castoff
as a guitarman plays.

Little fingers hold the tremolo
and Honolulu beckons,
surfboard sketching faint
lovehearts in the sand.

And the fishquay
spoons the world
in its tender hands
and sings Moon River
to no one and everyone,
while Hank's old eyes
sparkle like rain
pattering on paving.

Stripping years away
as the cafe hums
and a pensioner strums
on a perfect Saturday. //

A Moment on the Stairs

Bentbacked, drinkfaced, walkingsticked.
Unready, unsteady
he teeters at the summit.

A fat girl, fifteen years younger,
kindhand of unwelcome stability.

Bliddy hell woman!
What's wi' aall the fuss, like!?

His shaking head is stilled by
I love you.

A beat lasting all his life.

A foreverlook
and he turns sheep.

Aye...well...

She walks him through the door
and out into the future. ⁄⁄

The Different Boy

He was The Different Boy,
a shortofbreath sprinter
who only ever ran away.

A pyrotechnic wrangler,
moonbursting star sprinkler
who couldn't work a lighter.

Who could blush to order
if the order was to speak,
but who ran into spotlights.

And shy bairns get no sweets,
but he always kept a stash
in the contradiction tin.

No cruising on main roads,
bottlenecked with logic;
took the path marked *quicksand*.

Serial settle downer,
with the emphasis on down;
the Duke Of Optimism,
holy pants and borrowed crown.

Fat then thin and back again.
Shameless whilst ashamed.
Fulloffun and yet somehow
empty. ⫽

Chapter 4 – Running In

Time and Tide

We built the world, every metropolis
came from Ironopolis – Ian Horn
Well so fucking what? – Harry Gallagher

Your bridges stand corroded by weather
and years; and the leather hands
that hammered them into shape
are now decades underground.

And your train cracked rails,
slowly rusting away,
are gradually replaced
by the cheaper and newer.

And the families of those woodbine men,
who were hewn from the rock in the hills,
are now brushed away by the North winds,
whipping incessant from the sea.

The decrepit shell of the works,
a lone and lonely skeletal
reminder of the fickleness
of time and tide. ⁄⁄

Northern Poorhouse

Jackie Milburn picks up dog ends
on the high level bridge, beneath
the all seeing stare of Stephenson.

Joseph Swan drinks Carlsberg Export,
huddled on a pavement mattress
outside the Holy Jesus Hospital.

Bobby Charlton smokes his last
in bed, red all over his face;
no consolation goal, no-one to see.

While darling Grace saves tins
for the food bank at Sainsbury's,
manna for wayfarers in distress.

The next great inventor of steam traction
has now given up on any further action
and works in the Sky call centre. ⁄⁄

World's End

Was it fate or history
that tacked us fast here,
in this tumbledown town
at the edge of creation?

You just keep running until
the road has run out
and the walls have built
themselves around you.

Then decades stripaway
every ounce of otherness,
until you are the bricks
and crumbling mortar.

Unable to leave, yet
no stomach for swimming,
as the faded facades
hold you tight as ice.

So you sing for freedom
and cry for a future
that came unbidden
to the staithes at World's End. ⁂

Steeltown

In streets erected for Steelmen,
now corroding away amidst
brickdust and graffiti;
and *Shazza luvs Ali,*
and derelict takeaways
that deliver to no-one.

And brokendown bicycles
carry ghosts of children.
All lost forever in these streets
laid out for long dead Steelmen,
whose kids trudged in their footsteps
and pledged their allegiance
from cradle to grave.

And the boxes thrown up
in runaway time are now
haunted by spirits
from the furnace's ashes;
home to those whom
the steelworks abandoned.

Living out their lives on the CCTV,
which hangs from the lampposts
their forefathers forged,
in the town where the world was made. ⁄⁄

Replacement Therapy

Outside the church, with all
the other middle class aspirant
mothers, perfectly turned out
for respectable inspection.

Alongside the tweeds, nylons
and leather uppers; with the sermon
about that camel wedged in needle's eye
fast fading in the distance.

And it never did leave you,
that power of hollow judgement,
the sure havoc it would wreak
should you ever be found wanting.

Until one day, suddenly frail
and old, we discovered
your mountain of clothes
blockading the wardrobe door.

Unworn treasures filling
a decades wide void
that we had created
by just leaving home. ⁄⁄

Old Man Joe

Jose Perez, Summer son of Basque,
accent never thinner than treacle,
wedded to each bone grinding task.
Master grafter, man of the people.

Franco defying mini renegade,
chewing up Lorca and starvation fags,
dog earing every juicy page.
Deep as a river or his face's crags.

It was as if all that Spanish sun
of a boyhood spent working the field
had powered a motor which spun and spun,
light leaking through face but body sealed.

While factory boys read their page threes,
a headshake from the don of taste.
A cackle, a look and *lovely bodies*
without de mind are a fackin' waste!

Always travelled light, did old man Joe;
lived in peace and died without fuss.
An unmarked plot in a quiet meadow
for an educated man. One of us. ⁄⁄

Whatever Happened to The Tuxedo Princess...?

Newcastle, we have your Princess.
She is orange and drowning
in a river gone bad. Leaning
into a tide only going out.

Snared by a bridge nobody uses;
she was old and decrepit,
skin seared brittle. Fell into
sludge's soft loving tug.

We have sponged her banal
with sunshine tomorrows, ashamed
to call the breakers in earshot.
She is almost bloated enough now.

And one day soon, we will bubble
about dignified ends; add her name
to the list of the glorious dead
of a town where everything dies. ⁄⁄

How to Kill A Giant

Slings and arrows are not what is needed,
there will be no blood let today;
rather, he must be softened over decades,
brought to understand that time is a thief.

Concern and moist words, shaking of heads
should be the order of the day
and gentle reminders to his grieving children
that he had become a relic.

Downplay the fire still in his guts
and the legs still striding oceans.
Bring the mourners together on the beach
to see the old man for one last wake.

Show them the ghosts of Newport Staithes,
let them drink to the Bell Brothers
in the shimmering frame of The Ruin.
Let their tears extinguish the furnace.

You kill a giant with sympathy
and the sly withdrawal of his food. ⁄⁄

Miss Ellerby

Miss Ellerby briefly played piano
beneath fast flickering film;
a life in black and white,
her Henry having succumbed
to the guns of Passchendaele;
a crimson crotchet
on a swaying stave.

And when the pictures started talking,
this redundant ivory charmer
became piano teacher extraordinaire.
Day and night breathing life
into the bodies of work
of long dead composers.

Month after year, stretching her patience
and her cardigan elbows
on Mozart resistant children
and sausage fingered heretics,
until Evensong was played for her
by a pianist she'd never heard of.

And the kids-turned-adults, who had
called her a witch, and had sucked painfully
on the Benelyn flavoured bricks she dished
out as boiled sweets, gathered to share our stories.

And the spine tinglers
which flowed from her
anytime we'd listen
were held like fragile lovers.

For as we looked at our fingers
dancing over invisible keys
the truth was revealed,
scarier than any ghoul:

that the old witch had seeped
her magic through knuckles and skin,
for all the time we'd sniggered behind hands
the spell had been sinking in. ⁄⁄

Heritage Centre

Throw another log on the fire Dad,
a new heritage centre is opening.

They'll put out the furnace
and pull up the rails,
let in the ramblers
on Sunday morning trails.

Put signs on the black path,
pointing to the museum,
shut up the salamander
in a steel mausoleum.

Take the last slabs off the rolls Dad,
and pour away the last of the pig.

Put photos on the walls
of the things that we made,
show them where the empire's
foundations were laid.

For bridges and buildings
will all disappear;
now unlock the gates,
our public are here. ⧵

Cullercoats Lullaby

Tonight's mercurial moon
glistens down benevolent
on the tiny seaside town,
as the silvering surf dances,
answering her partner's pull.

Soon she will be spent,
swooning at rockpools, whose
sideway steppers tango toward
deep blue black beneath
the shimmering silver.

Soon all will be lonesome
on the glimmering slipway,
as the wintery waters give
up their grip, frostbitten
fingers following the fishermen.

As the foghorn's lament
puts an arm around midnight,
The Crescent spits out its
last drops of drinkers, linked
arms steadying jellyfish feet.

And pitchdark is reclaimed
by frosty foxes, deathly
silence of owls falling
through air; parachuted
by magick, stealthy as swoops.

A morose taxi growls dogged,
rattling the tarmac;
a two o'clock prowl
for fares never there,
street empty as a driver's bed.

And now the death before day
and the burnout of streetlights;
salmon leaping into cloud,
unlocking the paintbox
just beyond the horizon.

A rosy blow on the cheeks
of sleeping policemen, doctors,
teachers and an unlikely hero,
as the streetsweeper winks
and kisses the day good morning. //

Old English Oak

Rooted in the wonder of *Where am I from?*
his feet gripped the earth 'til his toes grew tendrils.
Planted himself well in fertile ground;
refuged and nourished his space in the wood.

Each season was greeted with an upturned gaze,
from Winter's freezer to Summer's marigold haze.
And when time at last took his frayed old bark,
his saplings had strengthened beneath his canopy arms.

And though they bestrewed, as life always will,
they would always remain soft in his shadow. ⧸

Other anthologies and collections available from Stairwell Books

For further information please contact rose@stairwellbooks.com

www.stairwellbooks.co.uk
@stairwellbooks

—